"We desperately need a grass-roots m[...] book will help make it happen."
George Verwer, International Direc[...]

"Well-aimed, diverse, creative, and useful. This resource applies to all ages, and all kinds of believers and churches. Thanks to Geoff, a global Christian!"
William Taylor, World Evangelical Fellowship

"When it comes to personal involvement in the church's mission, most people know they should do something - they just don't know what! This book will deal with that problem."
Stuart Briscoe, Senior Pastor, Elmbrook Church,
Waukesha, Wisconsin

101

Ways to Change
Your World

Geoff Tunnicliffe

LITERATURE

WAYS TO 101
CHANGE
YOUR WORLD

©1997 by Geoff Tunnicliffe
Reprinted 2000

ISBN 1-884543-47-2

Cover Design: Paul Lewis

Printed in Colombia
Impreso en Colombia

About the Author

Geoff Tunnicliffe leads the Task Force for Global Mission of the Evangelical Fellowship of Canada, serves on the executive board of the World Evangelical Fellowship Missions Commission and is a faculty member for the Arrow Leadership Program.

In addition, he serves as Senior International Consultant for International Teams, a multi-national, team-based ministry serving in 33 countries.

As president of International Teams of Canada from 1988 to 1996, he led the organization in growing from involving less than 100 to over 700 short and long-term missionaries annually.

As a frequent speaker at church and college mission conferences, Geoff seeks to envision and motivate Christian believers to actively participate in the global mission of the church.

Geoff lives in Burnaby, British Columbia with his wife, Jewel, and their two children, Justin and Natasha.

Acknowledgements

101 Ways to Change the World is a project for which I have many people to thank:

- Deep appreciation goes to David Horton who really believed in this project and facilitated its development.
- I so appreciate the wonderful folks Charlie Victor. I am especially grateful to Greg Clouse, who helped me to expand and refine the contents, and for the editorial help of Barb Williams.
- To my colleagues and friends at International Teams, as well as our partners in ministry, I say thank you for your encouragement and prayers.
- To Kevin Dyer, my mentor, I say thanks for believing in me.
- I would like to add thanks to Karen Fagan who assisted in doing the research of the Global Snapshots.
- And finally, to my wife, Jewel, to whom I dedicate this book, I say thanks for your love and your commitment to the global mission of Christ. You have been a true example of a world Christian to me and to our children, Justin and Natasha.

The "Great Commission"

"Therefore go and make disciples of all nations,
baptizing them in the name of the Father, and of the Son, and of the Holy Spirit,
and teaching them to obey everything I have commanded you. And surely I will be
with you always, to the very end of the age."
Matthew 28:19-20

A call to become a world changer!

The challenge to "go, give, or pray" rings out from church pulpits and missions conferences around the country. But while Christians often leave these meetings inspired and ready to act, many have no clear direction as to where to begin, or what they can do specifically, even in their own neighborhood or community. Changing the world is a tall order!

On the following pages, you will find 101 simple, specific action steps that can help you follow through on your desire to be a world changer, a "Great Commission" Christian. Warning: don't try to accomplish everything at once! Instead, treat this book like a menu and select just five to seven of the suggestions. Then decide on a time frame (e.g. three, six, twelve months) and take action! You may want to accomplish several easy steps before moving on to the more difficult ones. Check out the resources listed at the end of the book. They will help you implement the action steps you have decided on.

Bringing the light of the Gospel to a world in darkness is too great a task to be accomplished by just a few. The entire body of Christ must get involved. But it can start with you, and it can start today. May the Lord help you as you step out to change the world!

Next to each idea you will find a symbol indicating the degree of difficulty for that idea. The easiest ideas are marked by a (♦); the medium hardest are marked with a (♦♦); and the hardest are marked with a (♦♦♦). Obviously it would not be wise to pick all your choices from the most difficult ideas. It would be too easy to get discouraged.

*R*ead a missionary biography;
find out how others got involved in
changing the world.

Global Snapshot

It is estimated that 120 million people are presented
with the Gospel for the first time each year.

2

*E*ncourage people to bring international food and share a meal together as a church or small group. During this time, pray for the needs of the cultures represented.

Global Snapshot
Over 55 million Chinese live outside of China.

*V*olunteer at a local rescue
mission or food bank.

Global Snapshot

The countries where the richest 20 percent of the world's population lives control
83 percent of the gross world product.

4

───── ─────

*P*ray for someone
in mission work.
Start with one person.

─────

Global Snapshot
There are 6.5 million Christian workers worldwide.

*R*ead an introductory missions
book. Discover what world
missions is all about.
(See Resource section for suggestions.)

Global Snapshot

There are 4,000 mission boards and 21,000+ service agencies in the world.

6

*S*ponsor a needy child through a Christian relief agency.

Global Snapshot

More than 6.5 million children under 5 years of age die each year from hunger related causes.

*D*iscover the world via the Internet.
Places to begin: The World Fact Book
or News Resources.
(See Resource section for details.)

Global Snapshot

It is estimated that the number of computers in Christian use will
grow from 400 million today to 2.5 billion by the year 2025.

*T*ake an evangelism training course
in your local church. If none is offered,
suggest *Becoming a Contagious Christian*
(Bill Hybels and Mark Mittelberg,
Zondervan) as a teaching resource.

Global Snapshot

Despite an overall growth trend in the numbers of Christians, the
percentage growth is declining proportionate to the world population growth.

*P*ut your loose coins in a jar each
day. At the end of the month give
what you have collected
to a worthy cause.

Global Snapshot

It is estimated that by the year 2025, 35% of the world's population
will have trouble getting fresh water.

*E*ncourage individuals, families, Sunday School classes, or home groups in your church to "adopt" a missionary.

Global Snapshot

Responsiveness to the Gospel is growing across the Arab Muslim World. In Algeria the number of believers has increased from 1,200 in 1979 to 12,000 in 1999.

*R*ead *National Geographic* and
other travel magazines
to learn more about the world.

Global Snapshot

By the year 2025, 60 percent of the world's people will live in Asia.

Keep the world visible; put up
a world map! Buy gadgets, T-shirts,
novelties, etc. with a world map
on them.

Global Snapshot
There are over 6 billion people in the world.

*H*elp an elderly neighbor with a
difficult project such as shoveling
snow, washing windows,
or cleaning gutters.

Global Snapshot

Twelve percent of North Americans are over sixty-five years old.

*A*s you hear of major world events
(terrorism, revolutions, typhoons,
earthquakes, etc.) make prayer
your immediate response.

Global Snapshot
In armed conflicts today, 90 percent of the casualties are civilians.

*R*ead a missions storybook to a child.

Global Snapshot

One hundred million children live on the streets of the world's cities.

Go on a prayer walk in your
neighborhood or city.
As you pass by, pray for people
in their homes or businesses.

Global Snapshot

Tokyo, Japan is the most expensive city in the world.
Dehli, India is the least expensive.

*R*ead the world news section of
Time, *Newsweek*, or *Maclean's*
magazine. Learn about events in
other parts of the world.

Global Snapshot

By 2015, 20 of the 25 largest cities will be in developing countries.

*P*ray for Christians who are
persecuted for their faith.

Global Snapshot
It is estimated 165,000 Christians will be martyred this year.

*J*oin the missions (or International Ministries) committee in your church. If a committee doesn't exist, consider forming one.

Global Snapshot

The Christian population in Nepal exploded from 25 believers in 1960 to 400,000 today.

Buy products made by poor people in developing countries.

Global Snapshot

Seven hundred million women and children are exposed to air pollution equal to smoking three-four packs of cigarettes a day. (Most of this pollution is caused through using open fires for cooking and heating.)

*T*ake an "urban plunge". Go to a city
and be an explorer rather than a tourist.
(Experiment: initiate conversations with people
from other countries or ethnic origins.)

Global Snapshot

By the year 2025 it is estimated 62 percent of all Christians will live in urban areas.

*J*oin a ministry team at a world-class event such as the Olympics, World's Fair or the Commonwealth Games.

Global Snapshot
Nine hundred million Christians regularly listen to Christian radio and TV.

*R*each out to the world that has come to you! Get involved with international students in your community.
(Idea: consider hosting a special meal during a holiday season.)

Global Snapshot

There are an estimated 800 ethnic groups living in the United States.

24

*H*old a garage sale and give the
proceeds to a worthy ministry.

Global Snapshot
By the year 2025 it is estimated that nearly 27% of the world's population
will live in squatter areas.

*H*elp sort and pack donated
goods for a food pantry
or Christian relief agency.

Global Snapshot

Each year more than 84,000 people are killed in earthquakes.

25

*S*tage a musical or drama
at your church that promotes
cross-cultural ministry.

Global Snapshot
In Iran more Iranians have come to Christ since the Muslim fundamentalist
revolution in 1979 than in the previous 1,000 years.

Show your commitment to the environment. Set up a "recycle shop" in your church where people in your community can bring good used clothes, appliances, and furniture for resale.

Global Snapshot

In North America, we throw away 44 billion metal cans, 28 million bottles, and 70 billion bottle caps annually.

*T*ry to learn the language
of a different ethnic group in your
community. Begin with just a few
phrases of greeting.

Global Snapshot
Today as many Christians in the world speak Spanish as speak English.

*S*ubscribe to a mission agency periodical or newsletter. *Pulse* is a great general newsletter.

Global Snapshot

There are nearly 1.2 billion Muslims in the world.

*L*earn about places of the world;
become an expert in the blue (geography)
section of Trivial Pursuit®.

Global Snapshot

Between 1989 and 1998 the Islamic population in Europe grew by over 100%.

*U*se *Operation World,*
a daily handbook for praying
for the world.

Global Snapshot

On average, a child born in the West will consume about thirty times more
in his lifetime than a child born in the two-thirds World.

Visit a local mosque or temple
and observe the activities
of the participants.

Global Snapshot

Islam is one of the fastest growing religions in the world.

*R*ead *Rich Christians in an Age of Hunger, Living on Less and Liking it More,* or other books on simplifying your lifestyle. Determine what changes you can make in order to free up more resources for ministry.

Global Snapshot

Over 1 billion people live on less than $1 U.S. per day.

34

*V*olunteer with a ministry that serves prisoners and their families. Contact Prison Fellowship International.

Global Snapshot
Each year organized crime costs $600 billion.

*P*ray for your church's
missionaries and
evangelistic outreach.

Global Snapshot

There are an estimated 4,250 billion hours spent in evangelism each year.

Attend a cultural event in your community.

Global Snapshot
By the year 2030, is estimated that 18.9 percent of the U.S. population
will be of Hispanic origin.

*E*nroll in a class on global
missions at a nearby Christian
college, or take such a course
by correspondence.

Global Snapshot

By the year 2025 it is estimated there will be over 1 billion Hindus.

*P*lant a tree.
It will help to remove "greenhouse
gasses" from the atmosphere.

Global Snapshot
Each year, 3.2 million acres of potential farmland in Africa are turned
into desert.

*L*earn about mission issues through
an Internet "Newsgroup" or "Forum".
Brigada is a good place to begin.
(See Resource section for details.)

Global Snapshot

20% of the world's primary age school children do not attend school.

*H*elp support a short-term or summer missionary.

Global Snapshot
The Jesus Film has been dubbed in 592 languages. Nearly 4 billion
people have seen the film worldwide.

*T*ake the *Perspectives on the World Christian Movement* course for in-depth teaching on the biblical, historical, cultural, and strategic issues of world missions. Classes are offered throughout the world.

Global Snapshot
More than 66% of the world's refugees are Muslims.

*A*dopt a country or specific
people-group for one year and focus
your prayers on that country or group.

Global Snapshot

Eighty-five percent of the world's poorest nations are located in the
least-evangelized part of the world.

*V*isit an area of your city (or a city nearby) that has a different ethnic makeup than your own community. Observe how different things are from where you live.

Global Snapshot

90 million Americans claim African, Hispanic, Asian or Native American ancestry.

*B*egin an evangelistic Bible study in your home for non-Christian friends. The Alpha Course, distributed by Cook Church Ministries has an excellent step-by-step friendly approach.

Global Snapshot

In Britain, there are 30,000 Christian clergy and more than 80,000 registered fortune-tellers.

*H*elp provide a Bible
for a needy Christian
in a restricted-access country.

Global Snapshot

Only 1 percent of the Scriptures distributed are directed
toward the least evangelized in the world.

*L*earn about the needs of refugees
in your community
and find out how you can help.

Global Snapshot

There are 50 million refugees and displaced people in the world.

*E*ncourage your children
(or a student you know)
to consider foreign exchange
student opportunities.

Global Snapshot

In Kenya 42 percent of the children work full- or part-time.

*C*orrespond with a missionary through e-mail.

(Caution: for missionaries living in countries that restrict religious expression, inquire about communication guidelines and cost first.)

Global Snapshot

The cost of telecommunications is less and less related to the distance of the communication.

*V*isit a different ethnic church in
your community and participate
in its worship service.

Global Snapshot

It is estimated by the year 2030, 6.6 percent of the U.S. population
will be of Asian origin.

*O*rganize a rich person/poor person lunch.
Provide three-fourths of the participants
(randomly selected) with small amounts of rice
and vegetables, and the other one-fourth with a
full course meal. Watch the reaction!

Global Snapshot

Rescue missions in North America serve over 28 million meals annually.

Consider a short-term ministry experience in another culture.

Global Snapshot

Unless someone goes to share with them, over 1.1 billion people have little chance of hearing the Gospel.

*C*ontribute to the administration
costs of a ministry. This helps
provide essential logistical support
for "front-line" activities.

Global Snapshot

It is estimated that 15% to 20% of the world has never had a fair chance
to hear the Gospel.

*L*eave a gift to a ministry in your will.

Global Snapshot

Each year more than $53 billion is spent on gambling.

*C*ollect used eyeglasses and give them to a mission.

Global Snapshot

A high percentage of those who have not heard the Gospel are also poor.

*A*ccept a job opportunity
overseas.

Global Snapshot

Over 3 million people a year die from tuberculosis.

*U*se a daily prayer guide.
Many mission agencies have them.

Global Snapshot

Korean churches have more than 6000 missionaries serving around the world.

*B*egin a "homework" club and tutor non-native students.

Global Snapshot

Thirty-six percent of African-American children live with both their parents.

*E*ncourage students to attend major mission events such as the triennial Student Mission Advance (Hamilton, ON) or the triennial Urbana Missions Conference (Urbana, IL).

Global Snapshot

Over 194,000 students have attended Urbana Missions conferences since they first began.

*P*rovide some of the
transportation costs for
shipping emergency relief supplies.

Global Snapshot

Nearly 40% of Colombia's 17 million young people live in poverty.

Do an act of service without anyone knowing what you are doing.

Global Snapshot

Just less than 50 percent of the world's families live
on an annual income of $4,500 or less.

*D*evelop a ministry to the hearing impaired in your community.

Global Snapshot

In North America over 23 million people have hearing impairments.

*P*ray for government leaders around the world.

Global Snapshot

Each year $150 billion is spent on drug trafficking.

*G*ive homemade Christmas
presents and send the money
you save to a needy orphan
or a homeless shelter.

Global Snapshot

791 million people in poor nations and 31 million Americans
still face hunger as a fact of life.

*D*rive elderly or handicapped people or neighborhood children to doctor appointments, church, the bank, or the supermarket on a regular basis.

Global Snapshot
Nearly 2 million elderly Americans report having trouble with two or more activities of daily living.

*H*ost a missions video party in your home. Check with mission agencies for a list of videos you can borrow or rent.

Global Snapshot

In the last twenty years, 400 churches in London, England have been converted to mosques.

*W*rite elected government officials regarding moral and/or social issues that need to be addressed.

Global Snapshot

Fifty percent of the world's population is unable to vote.

*V*olunteer at a local crisis pregnancy center.

Global Snapshot

For every five births in the world there are two induced abortions.

*O*rganize a free carnival
for underprivileged kids
in your community.

Global Snapshot

Every day in America 2,200 kids drop out of school.

*S*hoot a video of needs in your community and show it to your church, Sunday School class, or Bible study group.

Global Snapshot

Over 1 million children join the sex trade each year.

*F*amiliarize a recently arrived immigrant with your city. Explain the transportation system, the schools, local laws, shopping, etc.

Global Snapshot
There are between 4-6 million Muslims in North America.

*O*rganize a "concert of prayer" among the churches in your community. Focus on various nations of the world.

Global Snapshot

Of the approximate 1 billion citizens of India, over 50% of children under age 15 suffer from malnutrition.

*S*upport a national worker
or theological student
in another country.

Global Snapshot

Christianity has exploded in China with an estimated 70 million Christians.

*A*dopt a "grandparent"
in a local nursing home; make that
person a part of your family.

Global Snapshot

In 1998 there were 34.4 million people age 65 or older. That number is
estimated to jump to almost 70 million by the year 2030.

*H*elp pay for the translation of the Bible or Christian books.

Global Snapshot
At least 2,000 languages still need Scriptures translated.

*S*end Christmas care packages
to missionaries. Plan ahead to find
out what they need or like.

Global Snapshot

It is estimated that one missionary in twenty, career or long-term, leaves the mission field
to return home every year. Of these, 71 percent leave for preventable reasons.

*T*each English as a Second Language
(ESL) to new immigrants
in your community.

Global Snapshot

Over 800 million adults are illiterate.

*A*s a businessperson, pledge a percentage of your profits to a worthy ministry.

Global Snapshot
By 2025, the estimated world population will be 8.6 billion.

*D*evelop a "family album" of missionaries you know. Include photos, field and furlough addresses, telephone numbers, description of work, birthdates, and other family information. Use the album as a guide for prayer and keeping in touch.

Global Snapshot

There are 925 million absolute poor in the world (211 million are Christians).

*V*isit a missionary in his or her field of work.

Global Snapshot

In the least-evangelized part of the world, every hour 10,700 children are born and 1,400 people die without hearing the Gospel.

*O*rganize the youth in your
church to participate in an inner-city
or ethnic ministry.

Global Snapshot

Three million children die each year from vaccine-preventable diseases.

*H*elp meet the needs of your community. Encourage your church to develop recovery groups for addictions to: alcohol, drugs, gambling, pornography, workaholism, and eating disorders.

Global Snapshot

In the typical church, the average annual budget allocated for local evangelistic efforts is 2 percent of its annual budget.

*H*ave a "welcome night" at
your church for recently arrived
immigrants in your community.

Global Snapshot
There are more than 405,000 Christian places of worship in the U.S.

*G*et your youth group to sponsor a special fund-raising event (e.g., a twenty-four-hour fast, community clean-up, car wash, etc.) and give the proceeds to someone in need.

Global Snapshot

Over 33 million people worldwide are living with HIV / AIDS.

*P*ray for Bible couriers taking the
Word of God to countries who
restrict or forbid its use.

Global Snapshot
Over 3 billion people are denied the freedom of teaching ideas.

*D*evelop a garden (alone, or with your group or church) and give the fresh fruit and vegetables to a local city mission.

Global Snapshot

In New York City, 75,000 people survive by rummaging through trash cans for food.

*F*ast one meal a week
and give the money you save
to a food bank.

Global Snapshot
There are more than 50,000 products in today's typical supermarket.

*A*dopt missionary children. Send letters, photos, birthday cards, etc. You could even offer housing when they are in college and their parents are still overseas.

Global Snapshot

Over 350 million school-age children are working.

88

*M*ake a room in your house
available to someone who needs a
place to stay for a short time.

Global Snapshot
There are over 22 million prostitutes in the world.

*A*s a family, give Christmas gifts to the children of a prison inmate.

Global Snapshot

Between 100 and 200 million children are estimated to be involved in slavery and child labor.

*A*s you read your local newspaper
and hear about local people in need,
see if you can help.

Global Snapshot
Only one out of three churches in North America offers any
formal evangelism training.

*S*end an entire team from your
church into a cross-cultural setting for
two weeks (or longer, if possible!)

Global Snapshot

Less than 5% of missionary activity is focused on those who have never
had the chance to hear the Gospel.

*A*s a businessperson, consider
forming a joint venture with a
Christian businessperson
in another country.

Global Snapshot
There are over 4,100 cities with more than 100,000 people.

*P*ray that your children
(or children you know) would seriously
consider missionary service.

Global Snapshot

Most people make faith decisions before they reach the age of twenty.

*T*elephone a missionary; overseas
calls are less costly than you may think.
(Just remember the time difference!)

Global Snapshot
You can call anywhere in the world for less than $10.

*E*ncourage your children
(or children you know)
to send gifts to a missionary family.

Global Snapshot

By the year 2025, 2.6 billion people will identify themselves as Christians.

*E*xplore the Internet for mission
service opportunities. Go to
www.netaccess.on.ca/fingertip
for the largest listings.

Global Snapshot

It is estimated there are over 10 million weekly prayer meetings in the world.

*P*ray for missionary children who are often vulnerable to illness, isolation, and even spiritual oppression.

Global Snapshot

The average North American wedding reception costs $7,000.

*S*end your pastor(s) or other key
church leaders on a missions
vision-building trip.

Global Snapshot

Christian magazine publishers say articles on missions and world evangelism
are the least read articles in their publications.

Sponsor a toy drive for
needy children in your community.

Global Snapshot

North Americans have a disposable income of almost a trillion dollars.

*H*ave a "coming home" shower for a retiring missionary.

Global Snapshot

The U.S. currently has the world's highest teenage pregnancy rate.

*P*ray to the Lord of the harvest
that He would raise up new
laborers to change the world!

Global Snapshot

It has taken 2000 years to translate Scripture into 2000 languages, yet there
are still 440 million people who do not have a sentence of the Bible
in their own language.

Resources

Missionary Biographies:

Amy Carmichael: Let the Little Children Come, Lois Hoadley Dick, Moody Press.

Bruchko, Bruce Olsen, Creation House.

Eric Liddell: The Hero of the 1924 Paris Olympics, Catherine Swift, Bethany House Publishers.

Eternity in Their Hearts, Don Richardson, Zondervan Publishing.

Guardians of the Great Commission: The Story of Women in Modern Missions, Ruth Tucker, Zondervan Publishing.

J. Hudson Taylor: A Man in Christ, Roger Steer, Harold Shaw Publishers.

Send Me! Your Journey to the Nations, Steve Hoke and Bill Taylor, WEF.

The Church is Bigger Than You Think!, Patrick Johnstone, Christian Focus.

The Shadow of the Almighty, Elisabeth Elliot, Zondervan Publishing.

Working Your Way to the Nations: A Guide to Effective Tentmaking, Jonathan Lewis, Editor, Intervarsity Press.

Children's Books and Resources

From Arapesh to Zuni: A Book of Bibleless People, Karen Lewis, Wycliffe.

God's Kaleidoscope: A Video for Children, Wycliffe Bible Translators.

Kids for the World: A Guidebook for Children's Mission Resources, Gerry Dueck, William Carey Library.

Missions Made Fun for Kids: Creative Ideas to Involve Children in Missions, Elizabeth Whitney Crisci, Accent/David C. Cook.

Mission Story Books for Young Readers, OMF Publishing.

You Can Change the World: Learning to Pray for People Around the World, Jill Johnstone, Zondervan Publishing.

Prayer Resources

Operation World: A Day-to-Day Guide for Praying for the World, Patrick Johnstone, Zondervan Publishing.

Prayer Evangelism, Ed Silvoso, Regal Books.
Praying Through the Window: A Thirty-One Day Prayer Guide, Caleb Project.
That None Should Perish: How to Reach Entire Cities For Christ Through Concerts of Prayer, David Bryant, Regal Books.
Touch the World Through Prayer, Wesley Duewel, Zondervan.

Mission Resource Books

50 Ways You Can Feed a Hungry World, Tony Campolo and Gordon Aeschilman, IVP.
Catch the Vision 2000, Bill and Amy Stearns, Bethany House.
The Great Omission, Roberston McQuilkin, Baker Book House.
How to Be a World Class Christian, Paul Borthwick, Victor.
Living on Less and Liking it More, Maxine Hancock, Victor.
A Mind for Missions, Paul Borthwick, NavPress.

Rich Christians in Age of Hunger, Ronald Sider, IVP.
Serving as Senders: How to Care for Missionaries, Neal Pirolo,
Emmaus Road International.
Stepping Out: A Guide to Short Term Missions, YWAM.

Music and Mission Resources

Artists In Christian Testimony. *A.C.T.* is a mission board and non-profit umbrella empowerment ministry for *arts ministry and missions specialists* who are doing the church's kingdom ministries worldwide. PO Box 395, Franklin, TN 37065-0395. www.actinternational.org

International Worship and Arts Network. An excellent resource organization that provides information on worship in global missions and encourages and enables musicians and artists to use their talents on the mission field. www.worship-arts-network.com

Scott Wesley Brown, PO Box 27146, San Diego, CA 92198-1146. Email: swibcare@aol.com

Periodicals and Newsletters

Evangelical Missions Quarterly and *Pulse*, Evangelical Missions Information Service, PO Box 794, Wheaton, IL 60189.

Global Prayer Digest, U.S. Center for World Mission, 1605 Elizabeth Street, Pasadena, CA 91004.

The Great Commission Handbook, Berry Publishing Services, 701 Main St., Evanston, IL 60202-9908.

Resource Organizations

Advancing Churches in Missions Commitment (ACMC) An organization that helps local churches focus on missions, ACMC offers global outreach products, conferences, seminars, consultancy, and networking. 4201 N. Peachtree Rd., Suite 300, Atlanta, GA 30341. www.acmc.org

Association of International Mission Services (AIMS) PO Box 64534, Virginia Beach, VA 23464. www.aims.org

Caleb Project   www.calebproject.org
   10 W. Drive Creek Circle, Littleton, CO 80120.
Center for Student Mission   www.gospelcom.net/csm/
   27302 Calle Arroyo, San Juan Capistrano, CA 92675.
Evangelical Fellowship of Mission Agencies (EFMA)
   4201 N. Peachtree Rd., Suite 300, Atlanta, GA 30341
Interdenominational Foreign Missions Association (IFMA)
   PO Box 398, Wheaton, IL 60189-0398. www.ifmamissions.org
Intervarsity Christian Fellowship Urbana Conference
   PO Box 7895, Madison, WI 53707-7895. www.urbana.org
Task Force for Global Mission, Evangelical Fellowship of Canada
   M.I.P. Box 3745, Markham, ON L3R 0Y4 Canada.
   www.globalmission.org
William Carey Library, Mission Resource Catalogue
   1605 Elizabeth St., Pasadena, CA 91104. www.uscwm.org

The Alpha Course Products, David C. Cook Church Ministries, 1-800-36-ALPHA. www.cookministries.com

The Christian Environmental Association, 1650 Zanker Road., Suite 150, San Jose, CA 95112. www.targetearth.org

Prison Fellowship International, PO Box 796009, Dallas, TX 75379. www.pfi.org

World Evangelical Fellowship Missions Commission, 4807 Palisade Dr., Austin, TX 78731. www.globalmission.org

Resources on the Internet

Brigada: www.brigada.org

Caleb Project: www.calebproject.org

Christian Information Network: www.christian-info.com

DAWN: www.jesus.org.uk/dawn/

Ethnologue: www.sil.org/ethnologue

Evangelical Fellowship of Canada: www.efc-canada.com

Evangelism and Missions Information Service of the Billy Graham Center: www.wheaton.edu/bgc/emis

Global Evangelization Movement: www.gem-werc.org

Global Mapping: www.gmi.org

Gospel and Our Culture Network: www.gocn.org

Gospel Communications Network: www.gospelcom.net

Global Connections: www.globalconnections.co.uk

Global Events Calendar: www.globalmission.org/calendar.htm

Global Opportunities Database: www.globalmission.org/go.htm

The International Conference on Computing and Mission: www.gospelcom.net/iccm/

Leadership Network: www.leadnet.org

Mission Network News: www.gospelcom.net

Mission America: www.missionamerica.org

United Nations High Commission for Refugees: www.unhcr.ch

Urbana: www.urbana.org
Willow Creek Association: www.willowcreek.com
World Evangelical Fellowship: www.worldevangelical.org
World Fact Book: www.odci.gov/cia/publications/pubs.html

Sources

Barrett, David and Todd Johnson. *AD 2000, Global Monitor.*

Barrett, David and Todd Johnson. *Our Globe and How to Reach It.* New Hope, 1990.

Campolo, Tony. *How to Rescue the Earth without Worshiping Nature.* Nelson, 1992.

World Population Data Sheet, Population Reference Bureau.

Henshaw, Stanley and Evelyn Morrow. *Induced Abortion: A World Review,* 1990. Supplement. The Alan Guttmacher Institute. 1990.

Logan, Robert and Larry Short. *Mobilizing for Compassion: Moving People into Ministry,* Fleming H. Revell.

Myers, Bryant. *The Changing Shape of World Mission.* MARC, 1993.

Myers, Bryant. *The New Context of Mission.* MARC, 1996.

UNHCR, State of the World's Refugees 1995: In Search of Solutions, New York: Oxford University Press.

Macleans Magazine, November 4, 1996.

Long, Justin. *Reality Check, Global Evangelization Movement.*

World PULSE, Evangelical Missions Information Service.

USA Today, January 20, 1997.

Target Earth Magazine, Christian Environmental Association, January 1997.

Leadership Magazine. Christianity Today, Inc.

Otis, George. *Strongholds of the 10/40 Window,* YWAM Publishing, 1995.

McClung, Floyd and Kalafi Moala. *Nine Worlds to Win,* YWAM Publishing, 1998.

Pirolo, Neal. *Serving as Senders,* Emmaus Road International, 1991.

Schmidt, J. David. *The Great Commission - Cause or Casualty?* ACMC, 1992.

Sjogren, Bob and Bill & Amy Stearns. *Run With the Vision,* Bethany House Publishers, 1995.

Reducing Missionary Attrition Project Consultation, World Evangelical Fellowship Missions Commission, 1996.

Send your ideas to change the world to:

Geoff Tunnicliffe
International Teams
1 Union Street
Elmira, Ontario N3B 3J9
Canada